Preface

Welcome to the CTET Paper 2 Class VI to VIII Science Book!

Teaching is a journey of learning, discovery, and personal growth. This book is designed to support you on that journey as you prepare for the Central Teacher Eligibility Test (CTET). Whether you are an aspiring educator or looking to enhance your knowledge, this book will equip you with essential concepts, strategies, and insights to excel in the exam and in your future teaching career.

Our goal is to make your learning experience meaningful and effective. Each chapter in this book has been carefully crafted to engage both your curiosity and critical thinking, covering core topics essential for the CTET exam. Along the way, you will find opportunities to reflect on best practices in education, the role of teachers in shaping society, and the importance of fostering an inclusive and supportive learning environment.

Wishing you success on your CTET journey!

Happy Learning!

Table of Contents

Chapter 1: Questions

1.**Which nutrient is essential for growth and repair of tissues?**

a) Carbohydrates

b) Proteins

c) Fats

d) Vitamins

Answer: b

2.**Which material is a good conductor of electricity?**

a) Wood

b) Plastic

c) Copper

d) Rubber

Answer: c

3.**Which part of a plant is responsible for photosynthesis?**

a) Roots

b) Stem

c) Leaves

d) Flowers

Answer: c

4.**What is the force that pulls objects toward the Earth?**

a) Magnetism

b) Gravity

c) Friction

d) Air resistance

Answer: b

5.**Which device converts electrical energy into mechanical energy?**

a) Battery

b) Generator

c) Electric motor

d) Transformer

Answer: c

6.**What is the function of an electric circuit?**

a) To generate light

b) To provide a path for electric current

c) To store electric charges

d) To block electric current

Answer: b

7.**What happens when like poles of two magnets are brought close?**

a) They attract

b) They repel

c) They lose magnetism

d) They become neutral

Answer: b

8.**What is the source of energy for the water cycle?**

a) Wind

b) Sun

c) Moon

d) Earth's gravity

Answer: b

9.**Which gas is essential for photosynthesis?**

a) Oxygen

b) Nitrogen

c) Carbon dioxide

d) Hydrogen

Answer: c

10.**What type of natural resource is solar energy?**

a) Non-renewable

b) Renewable

c) Fossil fuel

d) Limited resource

Answer: b

11.**What is the primary aim of science education?**

a) Memorization of facts

b) Understanding scientific concepts

c) Passing exams

d) Following instructions

Answer: b

12.**What does the structure of science involve?**

a) Collection of random facts

b) Concepts, principles, and theories

c) Memorizing equations

d) Creating diagrams

Answer: b

13.**Which teaching method emphasizes hands-on learning?**

a) Lecture method

b) Inquiry-based learning

c) Dictation method

d) Silent reading

Answer: b

14.**Why is creativity important in science education?**

a) It discourages logical thinking

b) It promotes innovation

c) It makes learning easier

d) It helps in memorizing concepts

Answer: b

15.**What is the role of evaluation in science education?**

a) To assign grades only

b) To assess learning and provide feedback

c) To discourage participation

d) To increase homework load

Answer: b

16.**Which organ in humans is responsible for pumping blood?**

a) Brain

b) Lungs

c) Heart

d) Liver

Answer: c

17.**What is a magnet made of?**

a) Plastic

b) Iron

c) Rubber

d) Wood

Answer: b

18.**Which planet is known as the 'Red Planet'?**

a) Mercury

b) Venus

c) Mars

d) Jupiter

Answer: c

19.**What is the energy stored in food called?**

a) Light energy

b) Heat energy

c) Chemical energy

d) Mechanical energy

Answer: c

20.**Which type of circuit allows current to flow through multiple paths?**

a) Series circuit

b) Open circuit

c) Parallel circuit

d) Short circuit

Answer: c

21.**Which component of soil is responsible for its fertility?**

a) Sand

b) Silt

c) Clay

d) Humus

Answer: d

22.**What is an example of a fossil fuel?**

a) Solar energy

b) Coal

c) Wind energy

d) Biomass

Answer: b

23.**Which scientific approach encourages students to explore and ask questions?**

a) Inquiry-based learning

b) Lecture method

c) Silent reading

d) Dictation method

Answer: a

24.**What is the purpose of science experiments in education?**

a) To memorize theories

b) To learn by doing

c) To avoid mistakes

d) To write essays

Answer: b

25.**How does innovation benefit science teaching?**

a) It makes learning monotonous

b) It introduces new methods and tools

c) It reduces student participation

d) It discourages creativity

Answer: b

26.**Which gas is released during photosynthesis?**

a) Carbon dioxide

b) Oxygen

c) Nitrogen

d) Hydrogen

Answer: b

27.**What is a renewable natural resource?**

a) Coal

b) Natural gas

c) Wind energy

d) Petroleum

Answer: c

28.**Which device measures electric current?**

a) Voltmeter

b) Ammeter

c) Thermometer

d) Barometer

Answer: b

29.**What is an essential property of magnets?**

a) They attract all materials

b) They attract only non-metals

c) They attract certain metals like iron

d) They repel metals

Answer: c

30.**How does friction affect motion?**

a) It speeds up objects

b) It stops objects in motion

c) It increases energy

d) It has no effect on motion

Answer: b

31.**Which is the largest organ in the human body?**

a) Liver

b) Brain

c) Skin

d) Heart

Answer: c

32.**Which energy source is used in solar panels?**

a) Wind energy

b) Solar energy

c) Geothermal energy

d) Hydro energy

Answer: b

33.**What is the main goal of science education?**

a) Memorizing scientific facts

b) Understanding and applying scientific knowledge

c) Copying information from textbooks

d) Writing long essays

Answer: b

34.**What is the role of creativity in scientific research?**

a) To make experiments complex

b) To develop innovative solutions

c) To reduce participation

d) To memorize theories

Answer: b

35.**How does science education help students?**

a) By promoting rote learning

b) By fostering curiosity and logical thinking

c) By reducing practical knowledge

d) By discouraging critical thinking

Answer: b

36.**Which phenomenon causes the change in seasons?**

a) Rotation of the Earth

b) Revolution of the Earth around the Sun

c) Movement of the Moon

d) Gravitational pull of the Sun

Answer: b

37.**What is the function of a battery in an electric circuit?**

a) To stop the flow of current

b) To store mechanical energy

c) To provide electrical energy

d) To reduce resistance

Answer: c

38.**Which nutrient is the primary source of energy for the body?**

a) Proteins

b) Vitamins

c) Carbohydrates

d) Minerals

Answer: c

39.**How do plants absorb water from the soil?**

a) Through leaves

b) Through stems

c) Through roots

d) Through flowers

Answer: c

40. **What is the purpose of evaluation in science education?**

a) To assign final grades only

b) To assess understanding and improve learning

c) To reduce student participation

d) To rank students in class

Answer: b

41. **Which force causes objects to fall to the ground?**

a) Friction

b) Gravity

c) Magnetism

d) Air resistance

Answer: b

42. **What is an example of a non-renewable resource?**

a) Wind energy

b) Solar energy

c) Coal

d) Water

Answer: c

43. **Which part of the plant conducts water and minerals?**

a) Roots

b) Stem

c) Leaves

d) Flowers

Answer: b

44. **Which device stores chemical energy and converts it to electrical energy?**

a) Generator

b) Transformer

c) Battery

d) Motor

Answer: c

45.**Which type of circuit allows only one path for electric current?**

a) Parallel circuit

b) Series circuit

c) Open circuit

d) Short circuit

Answer: b

46.**Which element is essential for the human body to produce hemoglobin?**

a) Iron

b) Calcium

c) Magnesium

d) Sodium

Answer: a

47.**What natural resource is used to produce paper?**

a) Metal

b) Plastic

c) Wood

d) Coal

Answer: c

48.**Which nutrient helps in strengthening bones?**

a) Vitamin C

b) Vitamin D

c) Vitamin A

d) Vitamin K

Answer: b

49.**What type of energy is produced by a moving object?**

a) Potential energy

b) Kinetic energy

c) Chemical energy

d) Thermal energy

Answer: b

50.**Which gas is needed for human respiration?**

a) Nitrogen

b) Oxygen

c) Carbon dioxide

d) Hydrogen

Answer: b

51.**How does a compass work?**

a) It uses the Sun's position

b) It aligns with Earth's magnetic field

c) It relies on gravity

d) It detects temperature changes

Answer: b

52.**Which natural phenomenon causes lightning?**

a) Earthquake

b) Air pressure differences

c) Electric discharge in clouds

d) Tidal waves

Answer: c

53.**What is the effect of friction on moving objects?**

a) It increases speed

b) It reduces resistance

c) It slows down the object

d) It converts energy to chemical form

Answer: c

54.**Which material is used to make electrical wires?**

a) Wood

b) Iron

c) Copper

d) Plastic

Answer: c

55.**How do humans obtain vitamin D naturally?**

a) Drinking water

b) Sunlight exposure

c) Eating fruits

d) Exercise

Answer: b

56.**Which simple machine is used to lift heavy objects?**

a) Pulley

b) Screw

c) Lever

d) Wheel

Answer: a

57.**Which organ in the human body filters blood?**

a) Stomach

b) Kidneys

c) Lungs

d) Heart

Answer: b

58.**Which type of rock is formed from molten lava?**

a) Sedimentary rock

b) Igneous rock

c) Metamorphic rock

d) Fossil rock

Answer: b

59.**Which form of energy is stored in food?**

a) Mechanical energy

b) Chemical energy

c) Thermal energy

d) Electrical energy

Answer: b

60.**What is the primary source of energy on Earth?**

a) Moon

b) Sun

c) Wind

d) Water

Answer: b

61.**What do plants release during photosynthesis?**

a) Oxygen

b) Carbon dioxide

c) Nitrogen

d) Hydrogen

Answer: a

62.**Which part of the plant helps it stand upright?**

a) Roots

b) Stem

c) Leaves

d) Flowers

Answer: b

63.**What causes the tides in oceans?**

a) Wind

b) Earth's rotation

c) Moon's gravitational pull

d) Sun's energy

Answer: c

64.**Which gas traps heat in Earth's atmosphere?**

a) Oxygen

b) Carbon dioxide

c) Nitrogen

d) Hydrogen

Answer: b

65.**Which nutrient provides insulation to the body?**

a) Carbohydrates

b) Proteins

c) Fats

d) Vitamins

Answer: c

66.**What is the role of chlorophyll in plants?**

a) It absorbs water

b) It gives flowers their color

c) It captures sunlight for photosynthesis

d) It stores food

Answer: c

67.**Which tool measures temperature?**

a) Thermometer

b) Barometer

c) Voltmeter

d) Compass

Answer: a

68.**What is the main purpose of science experiments?**

a) To memorize facts

b) To promote hands-on learning

c) To discourage mistakes

d) To reduce theoretical study

Answer: b

69.**What type of energy does a battery produce?**

a) Mechanical energy

b) Electrical energy

c) Thermal energy

d) Kinetic energy

Answer: b

70.**Which body system is responsible for transporting oxygen?**

a) Digestive system

b) Circulatory system

c) Nervous system

d) Respiratory system

Answer: b

71.**What do we call the energy generated by wind?**

a) Solar energy

b) Geothermal energy

c) Wind energy

d) Nuclear energy

Answer: c

72.**What is the function of roots in plants?**

a) To produce food

b) To absorb water and minerals

c) To attract pollinators

d) To capture sunlight

Answer: b

73. **Which property allows water to dissolve many substances?**

a) Magnetism

b) Adhesion

c) Polarity

d) Density

Answer: c

74. **Which device prevents electrical overloads?**

a) Resistor

b) Capacitor

c) Fuse

d) Switch

Answer: c

75. **What is the process of water vapor turning into liquid called?**

a) Evaporation

b) Condensation

c) Sublimation

d) Precipitation

Answer: b

76. **Which energy source is non-renewable?**

a) Wind energy

b) Solar energy

c) Fossil fuels

d) Hydropower

Answer: c

77. **What keeps planets in orbit around the Sun?**

a) Magnetic force

b) Gravity

c) Air resistance

d) Friction

Answer: b

78.**Which human organ helps in breathing?**

a) Brain

b) Lungs

c) Heart

d) Stomach

Answer: b

79.**What is the function of a simple circuit?**

a) To block the flow of current

b) To provide a path for current

c) To convert mechanical energy

d) To store energy

Answer: b

80.**Which gas is essential for combustion?**

a) Nitrogen

b) Oxygen

c) Carbon dioxide

d) Helium

Answer: b

Answer: c

86.**Which part of the brain controls balance?**

a) Cerebrum

b) Cerebellum

c) Medulla

d) Spinal cord

Answer: b

87.**What type of material is rubber?**

a) Conductor

b) Insulator

c) Magnetic

d) Transparent

Answer: b

88.**Which mineral helps in the formation of strong bones?**

a) Iron

b) Calcium

c) Magnesium

d) Potassium

Answer: b

89.**Which component of air is used by plants during photosynthesis?**

a) Nitrogen

b) Oxygen

c) Carbon dioxide

d) Hydrogen

Answer: c

90.**Which instrument is used to measure atmospheric pressure?**

a) Thermometer

b) Barometer

c) Hygrometer

d) Altimeter

Answer: b

91.**What happens to the magnetic field when a magnet is cut in half?**

a) It disappears

b) It remains the same in each half

c) It reverses

d) It becomes stronger

Answer: b

92.**Which nutrient is required to prevent night blindness?**

a) Vitamin C

b) Vitamin A

c) Vitamin D

d) Vitamin K

Answer: b

93.**What kind of mirror forms an image smaller than the object?**

a) Plane mirror

b) Convex mirror

c) Concave mirror

d) Transparent mirror

Answer: b

94.**What is the main function of the respiratory system?**

a) Pumping blood

b) Digesting food

c) Exchanging gases

d) Filtering waste

Answer: c

95.**Which device converts mechanical energy into electrical energy?**

a) Generator

b) Motor

c) Battery

d) Switch

Answer: a

96.**What is the unit of electric current?**

a) Volt

b) Watt

c) Ampere

d) Ohm

Answer: c

97.**What is produced when a candle burns?**

a) Water and oxygen

b) Carbon dioxide and water vapor

c) Hydrogen and nitrogen

d) Oxygen and carbon monoxide

Answer: b

98.**Which layer of the Earth is made up of molten rock?**

a) Crust

b) Mantle

c) Core

d) Atmosphere

Answer: b

99.**What force keeps the Moon in orbit around the Earth?**

a) Magnetic force

b) Air resistance

c) Gravity

d) Friction

Answer: c

100.**Which device allows electric current to flow in only one direction?**

a) Resistor

b) Diode

c) Capacitor

d) Switch

Answer: b

Chapter 2: Questions

101.**Which material can be recycled?**

a) Plastic bottles

b) Coal

c) Petroleum

d) Natural gas

Answer: a

102.**Which element is most abundant in the Earth's atmosphere?**

a) Oxygen

b) Nitrogen

c) Carbon dioxide

d) Argon

Answer: b

103.**What causes day and night on Earth?**

a) Earth's revolution

b) Earth's rotation

c) Gravitational pull of the Moon

d) Tilt of the Earth's axis

Answer: b

104.**Which nutrient helps in healing wounds?**

a) Vitamin A

b) Vitamin C

c) Vitamin D

d) Vitamin K

Answer: b

105.**Which type of wave is used in mobile communication?**

a) Sound waves

b) Radio waves

c) X-rays

d) Light waves

Answer: b

106.**What happens to water at 100°C?**

a) It freezes

b) It evaporates

c) It condenses

d) It becomes denser

Answer: b

107.**Which gas is used in fire extinguishers?**

a) Carbon dioxide

b) Oxygen

c) Hydrogen

d) Methane

Answer: a

108.**Which organ pumps oxygen-rich blood to the body?**

a) Brain

b) Heart

c) Lungs

d) Liver

Answer: b

109.**What is the primary function of chloroplasts in plant cells?**

a) Storing food

b) Capturing sunlight for photosynthesis

c) Providing structure

d) Absorbing nutrients from soil

Answer: b

110.**What type of energy is stored in a stretched rubber band?**

a) Kinetic energy

b) Thermal energy

c) Potential energy

d) Chemical energy

Answer: c

111.**What is a circuit with a broken path called?**

a) Closed circuit

b) Open circuit

c) Parallel circuit

d) Short circuit

Answer: b

112.**What are the primary colors of light?**

a) Red, blue, green

b) Red, yellow, green

c) Blue, black, white

d) Red, white, yellow

Answer: a

113.**What is the function of the digestive system?**

a) Filtering waste

b) Breaking down food for nutrients

c) Pumping blood

d) Controlling body temperature

Answer: b

114.**What causes objects to float in water?**

a) Friction

b) Gravity

c) Buoyancy

d) Magnetic force

Answer: c

115.**Which gas is used in balloons to make them float?**

a) Oxygen

b) Carbon dioxide

c) Helium

d) Hydrogen

Answer: c

116.**Which metal is liquid at room temperature?**

a) Iron

b) Mercury

c) Silver

d) Aluminum

Answer: b

117.**Which renewable resource is used to generate hydroelectric power?**

a) Coal

b) Water

c) Natural gas

d) Petroleum

Answer: b

118.**Which human organ produces insulin?**

a) Liver

b) Pancreas

c) Kidneys

d) Heart

Answer: b

119.**What is the main component of natural gas?**

a) Methane

b) Ethane

c) Propane

d) Butane

Answer: a

120.**What is the boiling point of water at sea level?**

a) 50°C

b) 75°C

c) 100°C

d) 120°C

Answer: c

121.**Which component of an electric circuit controls the flow of current?**

a) Battery

b) Switch

c) Resistor

d) Capacitor

Answer: b

122.**Which phenomenon causes objects to fall faster in the absence of air?**

a) Friction

b) Buoyancy

c) Gravity

d) Magnetism

Answer: c

123.**Which nutrient helps prevent scurvy?**

a) Vitamin A

b) Vitamin C

c) Vitamin D

d) Vitamin K

Answer: b

124.**What do we call the change of state from gas to liquid?**

a) Evaporation

b) Condensation

c) Sublimation

d) Freezing

Answer: b

125.**What kind of lens is used to correct farsightedness?**

a) Convex lens

b) Concave lens

c) Cylindrical lens

d) Plane lens

Answer: a

126.**Which organelle in plant cells stores water?**

a) Nucleus

b) Chloroplast

c) Vacuole

d) Mitochondria

Answer: c

127.**What is the SI unit of force?**

a) Joule

b) Newton

c) Watt

d) Pascal

Answer: b

128.**Which energy transformation occurs in a fan?**

a) Electrical to mechanical

b) Mechanical to electrical

c) Chemical to thermal

d) Light to chemical

Answer: a

129.**What type of rock is formed from compressed layers of sediment?**

a) Igneous rock

b) Sedimentary rock

c) Metamorphic rock

d) Lava rock

Answer: b

130.**What causes eclipses?**

a) Sun's rotation

b) Earth's revolution

c) Alignment of the Sun, Moon, and Earth

d) Tides

Answer: c

131.**Which part of the human brain controls thinking and memory?**

a) Cerebrum

b) Cerebellum

c) Medulla

d) Spinal cord

Answer: a

132.**Which gas makes up the majority of Earth's atmosphere?**

a) Oxygen

b) Nitrogen

c) Carbon dioxide

d) Hydrogen

Answer: b

133.**What is the effect of resistance in an electric circuit?**

a) Increases current

b) Reduces current

c) Stores energy

d) Converts energy into light

Answer: b

134.**Which material is used to make magnets?**

a) Copper

b) Rubber

c) Iron

d) Plastic

Answer: c

135.**What is the function of white blood cells?**

a) Transport oxygen

b) Fight infections

c) Regulate temperature

d) Store energy

Answer: b

136.**Which natural resource is most affected by deforestation?**

a) Fossil fuels

b) Soil fertility

c) Mineral resources

d) Water reserves

Answer: b

137.**Which energy source powers solar cells?**

a) Heat energy

b) Nuclear energy

c) Solar energy

d) Wind energy

Answer: c

138.**What is the role of mitochondria in cells?**

a) Photosynthesis

b) Store nutrients

c) Produce energy

d) Control cell division

Answer: c

139.**Which part of the flower produces pollen?**

a) Ovary

b) Petal

c) Anther

d) Sepal

Answer: c

140.**Which planet is the largest in the solar system?**

a) Mars

b) Earth

c) Jupiter

d) Venus

Answer: c

141.**What kind of charge does an electron have?**

a) Positive

b) Negative

c) Neutral

d) No charge

Answer: b

142.**Which phenomenon causes rainbows?**

a) Reflection

b) Refraction and dispersion

c) Evaporation

d) Condensation

Answer: b

143.**Which device is used to measure electric potential?**

a) Ammeter

b) Voltmeter

c) Barometer

d) Thermometer

Answer: b

144.**What type of energy is stored in a compressed spring?**

a) Kinetic energy

b) Thermal energy

c) Potential energy

d) Electrical energy

Answer: c

145.**Which organ in humans is responsible for detoxifying chemicals?**

a) Kidney

b) Liver

c) Lungs

d) Heart

Answer: b

146.**Which part of a plant transports food from leaves to other parts?**

a) Xylem

b) Phloem

c) Roots

d) Stem

Answer: b

147.**What causes a compass needle to point north?**

a) Earth's gravitational pull

b) Earth's magnetic field

c) Wind currents

d) Sunlight

Answer: b

148.**Which layer of the atmosphere contains the ozone layer?**

a) Troposphere

b) Stratosphere

c) Mesosphere

d) Thermosphere

Answer: b

149.**Which nutrient is essential for muscle growth?**

a) Protein

b) Carbohydrates

c) Fats

d) Vitamins

Answer: a

150.**Which planet is closest to the Sun?**

a) Venus

b) Earth

c) Mars

d) Mercury

Answer: d

151.**What is the boiling point of water at sea level in Fahrenheit?**

a) 32°F

b) 100°F

c) 212°F

d) 150°F

Answer: c

152.**Which metal is known as a good conductor of electricity?**

a) Iron

b) Copper

c) Gold

d) Aluminum

Answer: b

153.**What is the function of a fuse in an electrical circuit?**

a) Increase current

b) Protect the circuit from overload

c) Store energy

d) Generate electricity

Answer: b

154.**Which human organ helps maintain body temperature?**

a) Lungs

b) Brain

c) Skin

d) Liver

Answer: c

155.**What is the unit of energy in the SI system?**

a) Newton

b) Joule

c) Watt

d) Ohm

Answer: b

156.**What is formed when water vapor cools in the air?**

a) Snow

b) Clouds

c) Lightning

d) Wind

Answer: b

157.**Which process turns solid directly into gas?**

a) Evaporation

b) Condensation

c) Sublimation

d) Melting

Answer: c

158.**What is the pH value of pure water?**

a) 0

b) 7

c) 10

d) 14

Answer: b

159.**Which type of energy is produced by vibrations?**

a) Light energy

b) Sound energy

c) Heat energy

d) Nuclear energy

Answer: b

160.**What kind of current flows in one direction only?**

a) Alternating current (AC)

b) Direct current (DC)

c) Magnetic current

d) Static current

Answer: b

161.**Which nutrient is responsible for strong teeth and bones?**

a) Iron

b) Calcium

c) Vitamin C

d) Protein

Answer: b

162.**What is the chemical formula of water?**

a) CO_2

b) H_2O

c) O_2

d) NaCl

Answer: b

163.**What is the main function of red blood cells?**

a) Fighting infections

b) Transporting oxygen

c) Regulating body temperature

d) Producing hormones

Answer: b

164. **Which planet is known as the 'Morning Star'?**

a) Mars

b) Jupiter

c) Venus

d) Mercury

Answer: c

165. **What is the force that opposes motion between two surfaces?**

a) Gravity

b) Magnetism

c) Friction

d) Buoyancy

Answer: c

166.**Which layer of the Earth is the hottest?**

a) Crust

b) Mantle

c) Outer core

d) Inner core

Answer: d

167. **What kind of energy does a stretched bow have?**

a) Kinetic energy

b) Potential energy

c) Electrical energy

d) Thermal energy

Answer: b

168.**Which metal is used to make thermometers?**

a) Copper

b) Aluminum

c) Mercury

d) Iron

Answer: c

169. **What is the primary gas in the Sun?**

a) Oxygen

b) Hydrogen

c) Carbon dioxide

d) Helium

Answer: b

170.**Which natural phenomenon is caused by the Earth's rotation?**

a) Seasons

b) Day and night

c) Tides

d) Eclipses

Answer: b

171.**What do animals exhale during respiration?**

a) Oxygen

b) Nitrogen

c) Carbon dioxide

d) Hydrogen

Answer: c

172. **Which device is used to convert solar energy into electricity?**

a) Wind turbine

b) Battery

c) Solar cell

d) Generator

Answer: c

173.**Which element is essential for making proteins?**

a) Calcium

b) Iron

c) Nitrogen

d) Magnesium

Answer: c

174.**What is the main function of chloroplasts in plants?**

a) Store water

b) Capture sunlight for photosynthesis

c) Transport minerals

d) Produce proteins

Answer: b

175.**What is the name of the process by which plants release water vapor?**

a) Photosynthesis

b) Transpiration

c) Condensation

d) Precipitation

Answer: b

176. **What kind of lens is used in a magnifying glass?**

a) Convex lens

b) Concave lens

c) Plane lens

d) Cylindrical lens

Answer: a

177.**Which gas is used in the production of soft drinks?**

a) Oxygen

b) Carbon dioxide

c) Nitrogen

d) Hydrogen

Answer: b

178.**What is the study of animals called?**

a) Botany

b) Zoology

c) Ecology

d) Geology

Answer: b

179. **Which force allows birds to fly?**

a) Gravity

b) Buoyancy

c) Lift

d) Friction

Answer: c

180.**What is the common unit used to measure temperature?**

a) Newton

b) Joule

c) Watt

d) Celsius

Answer: d

181. **Which part of the human skeleton protects the brain?**

a) Spine

b) Skull

c) Ribs

d) Pelvis

Answer: b

182.**Which component of air is essential for combustion?**

a) Nitrogen

b) Oxygen

c) Carbon dioxide

d) Argon

Answer: b

183. **What type of energy is produced by moving water?**

a) Nuclear energy

b) Solar energy

c) Hydro energy

d) Thermal energy

Answer: c

184. **Which sense organ is responsible for hearing?**

a) Eye

b) Nose

c) Ear

d) Skin

Answer: c

185. **What is the function of the stomata in leaves?**

a) Absorb water

b) Exchange gases

c) Store food

d) Transport nutrients

Answer: b

186. **Which nutrient is needed to prevent anemia?**

a) Iron

b) Calcium

c) Vitamin C

d) Protein

Answer: a

187.**What is the speed of light in a vacuum?**

a) 3,000 km/s

b) 300,000 km/s

c) 150,000 km/s

d) 30,000 km/s

Answer: b

188.**Which planet is known as the 'Blue Planet'?**

a) Venus

b) Mars

c) Earth

d) Neptune

Answer: c

189. **Which part of the eye controls the amount of light entering?**

a) Cornea

b) Iris

c) Retina

d) Lens

Answer: b

190.**Which phenomenon makes the sky appear blue?**

a) Reflection

b) Refraction

c) Dispersion

d) Scattering of light

Answer: d

191. **Which organelle is known as the powerhouse of the cell?**

a) Nucleus

b) Mitochondria

c) Chloroplast

d) Ribosome

Answer: b

192. **Which organ in the human body produces bile?**

a) Liver

b) Stomach

c) Pancreas

d) Intestine

Answer: a

193. **Which type of mirror is used in car headlights?**

a) Plane mirror

b) Convex mirror

c) Concave mirror

d) Transparent mirror

Answer: c

194.**Which process involves the conversion of liquid to gas?**

a) Condensation

b) Evaporation

c) Sublimation

d) Freezing

Answer: b

195. **What is the main source of energy for the Earth?**

a) Moon

b) Sun

c) Wind

d) Water

Answer: b

196.**Which mineral is necessary for the functioning of nerves?**

a) Iron

b) Calcium

c) Potassium

d) Magnesium

Answer: c

197.**What happens to the shadow when the light source is closer?**

a) It disappears

b) It becomes larger

c) It becomes smaller

d) It changes color

Answer: b

198.**What is the unit of electric resistance?**

a) Volt

b) Ohm

c) Joule

d) Watt

Answer: b

199.**Which gas is released during cellular respiration?**

a) Carbon dioxide

b) Oxygen

c) Nitrogen

d) Methane

Answer: a

200.**What type of force pulls a magnet toward a metal object?**

a) Frictional force

b) Gravitational force

c) Magnetic force

d) Electrostatic force

Answer: c

Printed at Repro India Ltd.